If You Love the Lord

DAG HEWARD-MILLS

Parchment House

Unless otherwise stated, all Scripture quotations are taken from the King James Version of the Bible.

IF YOU LOVE THE LORD

Copyright © 2022 Dag Heward-Mills

First published by Parchment House 2022

Published by Parchment House 2022
1st Printing 2022

[77]Find out more about Dag Heward-Mills at:
Healing Jesus Campaign
Write to: evangelist@daghewardmills.org
Website: www.daghewardmills.org
Facebook: Dag Heward-Mills
Twitter: @EvangelistDag

ISBN: 978-1-64330-275-1

Contents

CHAPTER 1

If You Love the Lord:
You Are Doing the Most
Important Thing

MASTER, WHICH IS THE GREAT COMMANDMENT IN THE LAW? Jesus said unto him, Thou shalt love the Lord thy God with all thy heart, and with all thy soul, and with all thy mind. This is the first and great commandment...

Matthew 22:36-38

Do you love the Lord? That is an important question! Why is it an important question? Why is your love for God something that we need to discuss? From the scriptures, the most important thing we need to do is to love God.

1. LOVING THE LORD IS YOUR MOST IMPORTANT DUTY TO GOD.

MASTER, WHICH IS THE GREAT COMMANDMENT IN THE LAW? Jesus said unto him, Thou shalt love the Lord thy God with all thy heart, and with all thy soul, and with all thy mind. This is the first and great commandment. And the second is like unto it, Thou shalt love thy neighbour as thyself. On these two commandments hang all the law and the prophets.

Matthew 22:36-40

If you love the Lord you are doing the main thing. The most important thing! It is good that Jesus was asked the question, "What is the greatest commandment?" There are many commandments and instructions in the Bible. There are times you have to choose between the different instructions.

Should I pray? Should I fast? Should I witness? Should I teach the word? What exactly should I do? Should I wait on God? The single most important commandment ever given by Jesus is to love God. That is why loving the Lord is an important topic. That is why there is a whole book about it. That is why there are many things to be said about what you would do if you loved the Lord.

2. LOVING THE LORD IS THE PROPER RESPONSE TO GOD'S LOVE.

We love him, because he first loved us.

1 John 4:19

We love God because He first loved us. Love is supposed to provoke you to love more. Love is not supposed to provoke

2

silence, nonchalance, indifference, detachment and calmness in you. Love is supposed to spark a reaction of love from the recipient. We love Him because He first loved us!

You are supposed to be more in love with God as you think about His love for you. Indeed, if you love the Lord, it is because you are responding well to God's love. He loved you first! Respond properly and love Him back! Loving the Lord back is the right response to God's awesome love.

Unfortunately, some people do not respond properly to the love shown them. Some people take it all for granted. Others react by being afraid. What about if you lose this love one day? Others react by accusing their lover. Others react to great love by being unfaithful and presuming on the forgiveness of their partners. Yet still, there are others who repay your love with evil.

3. LOVING THE LORD IS THE BEST PREPARATION FOR JUDGMENT.

Herein is our love made perfect, that we may have boldness in the day of judgment: because as he is, so are we in this world.

1 John 4:17

If you love the Lord perfectly, you will be safe and even bold on the Day of Judgment. Your judgment will be based on "Question One". "Question One" is the most important question on your exam paper. "Question One" is the compulsory question. "Question One" carries more marks than all the other questions put together. Do you know what "Question One" is?

"Question One" is "Did you love the Lord?" All your judgment is going to centre on your love for God. If you love God, you will be bold on the Judgment Day.

You may have given an offering here and there whilst you were on earth. You may have donated to build a classroom block in your old school. You may have bought some bananas and pineapples for an orphanage in Africa. You may have sent an offering to support Ethiopian Jews migrating back to the Holy Land. But did you love the Lord?

Loving the Lord is very different from doing good works. It is when you get to heaven that your works will be assessed properly. The motives for what you did on earth will be uncovered. Did you do all that you did out of your love for God or did you do it to impress your fellow men? Did you send an offering to your church so that you would be acknowledged publicly or did you try to help the church out of your love for God?

4. LOVING THE LORD IS THE PROPER RESPONSE TO FORGIVENESS.

Wherefore I say unto thee, Her sins, which are many, are forgiven; FOR SHE LOVED MUCH: but to whom little is forgiven, the same loveth little.

Luke 7:47

Being forgiven is an amazing act of graciousness from Almighty God. When wrong things are done to you, you are affected mentally, psychologically, socially and emotionally. People who are harmed are often transformed by the grievous hurt that is inflicted on them.

Many films are based on this fact; people who are harmed by the events of life become revengers of evil. Do you not know a thousand films which are based on revenge for a wrong done? Many Chinese Kung-fu and karate films are based on revenge for a crime. Peaceful individuals are transformed into killers who seek revenge and justice throughout their lives.

I once watched a film in which a little girl saw her parents being killed and grew up to become an expert killer. You can never tell the harm you do to someone you hurt. People take things differently. Forgiveness is an unusual response to harm. Most people revenge or dream of revenge all through their lives.

Those who cannot avenge the evil done against them curse the evildoers from the bottom of their hearts. Many live and die

4

wishing to hear an evil report of something horrible happening to their enemies. Jesus came along with grace and truth. Jesus came to this world teaching us about forgiveness and love. He who is forgiven much loves much.

It is important to think of yourself as someone who has been forgiven much. Because God has forgiven you so much, it is important to spend your life loving and serving Him. I am sad to report that most Christians are glad to be forgiven for their sins but do not respond properly to God's love. Christians should have responded with a deep and passionate love for God.

But what do we see today? Churches filled with Christians seeking for things! Churches filled with Christians looking for marriage partners! Instead of seeking God and loving Him, we come to church seeking things and loving the world.

5. LOVING THE LORD IS THE EVIDENCE OF GOD'S PRESENCE.

And we have known and believed the love that God hath to us. God is love; and HE THAT DWELLETH IN LOVE DWELLETH IN GOD, AND GOD IN HIM.

1 John 4:16

When you dwell in God, you dwell in love! Loving the Lord is a sign that God is in you! Loving the Lord is a sign that the anointing of the Holy Spirit is in you. Why are you a Christian? Is it not because you are seeking God? Are you not seeking to know God and to find God in your life?

Indeed, you are! If you do not have the love of God, you have not found God. You claim that you are seeking for and searching for God. Have you found Him? If you have found God, He will be in you and with you.

God is love! If God is in you, you will have love. The love of God will fill you and dominate your life when you find God. Loving the Lord is the greatest proof of the presence of God.

6. LOVING THE LORD IS THE PROOF THAT LOVE CAN BE TAUGHT.

The aged women likewise, that they be in behaviour as becometh holiness, not false accusers, not given to much wine, teachers of good things; THAT THEY MAY TEACH the young women to be sober, TO LOVE THEIR HUSBANDS, to love their children, To be discreet, chaste, keepers at home, good, obedient to their own husbands, that the word of God be not blasphemed.

Titus 2:3-5

Love can be taught! If you love the Lord, it is probably because you have learnt to love him. You can learn to love him more! Love can be learnt! Love can be taught! You can learn to love the Lord. God is invisible! No one can see God! No one really knows how to love someone we cannot see. We are feeble and weak creatures.

We do not even know how to love our fellow human beings. However, we can embark on a project to learn how to love one another and also to learn how to love God.

Over the years, I have learnt how to love God. I have learnt how to relate with God whom I cannot see. There are scriptures that tell us exactly what to do if we want to love God. This whole book is about what to do if you really love the Lord.

You can learn anything. Many things can be learnt. Spiritual things can be taught.

Even obedience can be learnt as a subject. "Though he were a Son, yet learned he obedience by the things which he suffered" (Hebrews 5:8). Just as obedience can be learnt, love can also be learnt.

There is a notion that some things just come to us naturally. It seems as though you cannot learn how to love. When people get married, they are taught how to love one another. A man who does not actively learn how to love his wife will not be a good husband. A woman who does not actively learn how to love her

6

husband will fail in marriage. It is important to believe that you have to actually learn how to love.

7. LOVING THE LORD IS THE GOAL OF ALL MINISTRY.

But THE GOAL OF OUR INSTRUCTION IS LOVE from a pure heart and a good conscience and a sincere faith.

1 Timothy 1:5 (NASB)

THE PURPOSE OF MY INSTRUCTION IS THAT ALL BELIEVERS WOULD BE FILLED WITH LOVE that comes from a pure heart, a clear conscience, and genuine faith.

1 Timothy 1:5 (NLT)

Why are we teaching the word of God? Why are we ministering? What is the aim of all our pastoral work? What is the aim of all ministry? The aim of ministry is love. We are trying to get people to love God, which is the number one instruction. The biggest command from the Lord is to love Him. The goal, therefore, of all ministry, is to get people to love God.

Why are you experiencing all the things you are experiencing? What does God want for you? What is God trying to teach you? He is trying to teach you to love him. Some of the bad things you have experienced have been as a result of your failure to love God. The bombs in your life were allowed to happen to bring you to a place where you would love God and no one else.

The goal of God's instruction in your life is to get you to love the Lord. I have had some terrible experiences in my life. There are times I have wondered what God was trying to do in my life. I recognize today that all he has been doing is to get me to love Him with all my heart, with all my soul and all my strength.

He is trying to take my attention from those who are not worthy of my love and fix my heart on him alone. Do not be discouraged from the experiences you are going through. The goal of the instruction is love.

CHAPTER 2

If You Love the Lord:
You Will Obey Him

But those who obey God's word truly show how completely they love him. That is how we know we are living in him.

1 John 2:5 (NLT)

Obedience to God is the proof of your love for God. If you love the Lord you will keep His commandments. Love is a mysterious thing and it is not easy to express love. If it is difficult to show love to a human being whom you can see, how much more difficult is it to show love to a God you cannot see!

Some people give you a clue to loving them. There are people who say, "If you love me, show it by cooking good food for me." Some say, "If you love me, show it by smiling when you see me." Others say, "If you love me, give me a card with nice words." Still others say, "If you love me, "If you love me, take me out." Some say, "If you love me, take me for a walk." Some say, "If you love me, kiss me." Some others also say, "If you love me, chat with me." Some say, "If you love me, buy me chocolate." Others say, "If you love me, have sex with me. That is the only proof of their love."

Honestly, you may love someone with all your heart but your way of expressing love may be completely different from what the person perceives as love. It is therefore a blessing and a revelation when someone actually tells you what to do to show your love.

I once met someone who said, "If you love me, do this." I was completely taken aback by the person's request. I had no idea that such things constituted the expression of love.

God has been kind to us. God has declared that He feels our love when we obey Him. Obedience is God's love language! God has shown us a simple formula by which we can love Him. Indeed, the invisible God may be easier to love than some complicated human beings. He has shown us one thing that He recognizes as love: obedience.

Are you not glad that God would show you how to love Him? Are you not glad that God would actually spell out what to do to show your love for Him? God's word is clear: obey Him and you are loving Him!

The greater your obedience, the greater your love!

1. If you love the Lord, you will keep the word of God in your heart and then you will obey it.

But whoso keepeth his word, in him verily is the love of God perfected: hereby know we that we are in him.

1 John 2:5

You cannot obey the Word of God that is not in your heart. It is important to keep the word in your mind and in your heart. If something is not in your mind and your heart, you are not likely to do it. People hear the word of God but they do not keep it in their heart. You do not keep the word of God in your heart because you do not meditate on it. Meditation involves reading something over and over. When you pore over the word of God several times, you will discover that it will enter your heart and you are more likely to obey it.

2. If you love the Lord, you will keep His commandments which are not difficult.

The commandments of God are not grievous. As you go through life, you will discover for yourself that disobeying God is far more difficult than obeying Him.

Disobedience is far more grievous than obedience. Disobedience will lead you to sorrowing, regretting and mourning. Obedience will leave you elated and rejoicing at the goodness of the Lord.

For this is the love of God, that we keep his commandments: and his commandments are not grievous.

1 John 5:3

3. If you love the Lord, you will keep His commandments which you have received.

HE THAT HATH MY COMMANDMENTS, AND KEEPETH THEM, HE IT IS THAT LOVETH ME: and he that loveth me shall be loved of my Father, and I will love him, and will manifest myself to him.

John 14:21

He that has my commandments and does them is the one who loves me. God always makes sure that you receive His commandments. God makes sure that you get to know His will. Once you are aware of the will of God, you can no longer plead ignorance. There are many Christians who do not know certain things. Often, God winks at our ignorance. He ignores us because we are ignorant.

And the times of this ignorance God winked at; but now commandeth all men every where to repent:

Acts 17:30

Once you have his commandments you can no longer claim that you are ignorant of His will.

4. If you love the Lord, you will keep His commands from the scripture.

He that hath my commandments, and keepeth them, he it is that loveth me: and he that loveth me shall be loved of my Father, and I will love him, and will manifest myself to him. Judas saith unto him, not Iscariot, Lord, how is it that thou wilt manifest thyself unto us, and not unto the world? Jesus answered and said unto him, if a man love me, he will keep my words: and my Father will love him, and we will come unto him, and make our abode with him.

John 14:21-23

Where can you find the commandments of God? His commandments are found in the Holy Scriptures. You can also find the commandments of God through the Holy Spirit. Some people despise the reading of the Bible and do not consider it to be a powerful means of hearing from God.

If someone says, "Thus says the Lord" and wields a big face towel, they will consider that the prophet has spoken. Reading the Bible and seeing its simple instructions seems to be a much less supernatural way of hearing the words of God. After all, even unbelievers read the Bible sometimes. Many of the most significant turning points in ministry centred on a scripture that the Holy Spirit impressed upon me. I came into full-time ministry because I saw in the Holy Scripture the verse that said, "Give thyself wholly to these things." Nobody encouraged me, advised me or told me to give myself to full-time ministry. My daily Bible study was the source of my direction.

5. If you love the Lord, you will love and keep the instructions of the Father, the Son and the Holy Spirit.

He that loveth me not keepeth not my sayings: and the word which ye hear is not mine, but the Father's which sent me

John 14:24

The heavenly FATHER will speak to His children. He spoke to us through JESUS, "He that has seen the Son has seen the Father." He also speaks to us through the HOLY SPIRIT.

Be careful that you follow JESUS CHRIST closely. His life and His words are God's direction for your life.

Be careful, also, that you follow the HOLY SPIRIT. The Holy Spirit is the spirit of God. God is a spirit! If you respect the Holy Scripture, you must respect the Holy Spirit. Through the Holy Spirit, you will know the commandment and desire of the Father. You will show your love to God by continually obeying the Holy Spirit.

6. If you love the Lord, you will not listen to other voices, nor will you obey anyone in place of the Lord. Loving others instead of loving the Lord turns into a curse.

And it shall come to pass, if ye shall hearken diligently unto my commandments which I command you this day, to love the Lord your God, and to serve him with all your heart and with all your soul,

Deuteronomy 11:13

Whenever there is a third voice, a relationship is not secure. The Holy Spirit is one with the Father. He speaks of things He knows and things He has seen. Beware of the third voice. Any voice in your life that is different from the voice of God is the third voice which can take you astray.

And unto Adam he said, Because thou hast hearkened unto the voice of thy wife, and hast eaten of the tree, of which I commanded thee, saying, Thou shalt not eat of it: cursed is the ground for thy sake; in sorrow shalt thou eat of it all the days of thy life; Thorns also and thistles shall it bring forth to thee; and thou shalt eat the herb of the field;

Genesis 3:17-18

There are many third voices in this life. In Adam's situation, his wife was a third and dangerous voice to him. Eve destroyed the relationship that Adam had with God. Eve also had a good relationship with God. Eve would fellowship with the Lord God every day and in the cool of the day. The devil was the third voice that came in between Eve and her Lord.

I have had good relationships that were destroyed by the presence of a third party, a third voice and a third person. These third parties were lurking in the shadows, whispering and murmuring constantly behind my back. By their whisperings and mutterings, my good relationship with people was destroyed. Beware of third parties! Beware of the discontented characters waiting in the dark who fear to come out in the open and declare their true stance. Marriage in the law books is described as a relationship that exists to the exclusion of all others. Your marriage is not likely to succeed if you do not conduct it to the exclusion of others.

Who is destroying your relationship with God? Do not allow a third party to destroy your relationship with the Lord. Even a good person like a wife or a husband can become a third party and end up destroying your relationship with God.

In the Old Testament, God warns about these third voices and third parties. No matter how good and sincere these third voices seem to be, you must not listen to them if they are taking you away from God.

> **Thou shalt not hearken unto the words of that prophet, or that dreamer of dreams: for the Lord your God proveth you, to know whether ye love the Lord your God with all your heart and with all your soul.**
>
> **Deuteronomy 13:3**

7. **If you love the Lord, you will obey Him no matter what it costs you.**

> But thou, Israel, art my servant, Jacob whom I have chosen, the seed of Abraham my friend.
>
> Isaiah 41:8

Abraham was called a friend of God. Being a friend of God is not just a cliché. It is a real thing. Jacob was called the servant of God but Abraham was called a friend of God. Abraham obeyed God, even to the point of sacrificing his own son. To sacrifice your only son is not an easy thing. I once watched a film in which a man had a son who was murdered. The father of the son was asked, "How many people did you kill when your son was murdered." The father, in a rare show of emotion said, "when my son was killed I felt that my life had come to an end so I killed many people in response." Such remarks reveal the extreme love Abraham must have had for God, if he was ready to kill his son, Isaac.

Abraham was completely sold out to God. There was nothing that he would not do for the Lord. There was no third party between Abraham and God's relationship. Sarah could not come between Abraham and God. There was no adviser who came between Abraham and God. There was no friend who was lurking in the shadows of waiting in the dark to influence Abraham after he had had a meeting with God. Is it any wonder that God called him his friend?

Our God is a jealous God and He is constantly looking for someone who will love him as much as He loves us. There are many times I feel sad for God. God so loved the world that He gave His only begotten son to us. Yet we love Him so little. We are prepared to do very little for Him. We have not excluded many third parties from our relationship with God.

CHAPTER 3

If You Love the Lord: You Will Love the Brethren

If a man say, I love God, and hateth his brother, he is a liar: for he that loveth not his brother whom he hath seen, how can he love God whom he hath not seen? And this commandment have we from him, that HE WHO LOVETH GOD LOVE HIS BROTHER ALSO.

1 John 4:20-21

1. If you love the Lord, you will love the brethren.

If a man say, I love God, and hateth his brother, he is a liar: for he that loveth not his brother whom he hath seen, how can he love God whom he hath not seen? And this commandment have we from him, that HE WHO LOVETH GOD LOVE HIS BROTHER ALSO.

1 John 4:20-21

If you love the Lord, you will love the brethren. Your love for the people of God is the evidence of your love for God. You cannot see God but you can see your brothers in Christ. The human beings you love are an important test that determines whether you actually love God or not.

Whom you love and who you show affection for reveals what you love. There are people who love their families very much. There are people who love their sisters' children above their own children. I know someone who loved his sister's children so much that he gave away his properties to them.

There are people who love their political parties very much. Indeed, I know someone who loved his political party so much that he gave his property to his political party. Indeed, he had a great love for his political brothers and sisters. Many politicians consider their political parties as their families. You must love your spiritual family too. Your love for your spiritual family reveals your love for God. If you love the Lord, you will love your spiritual brothers and sisters.

2. If you love the Lord, you will lay down your life for the brethren.

Hereby perceive we the love of God, because he laid down his life for us: and we ought to lay down our lives for the brethren.

1 John 3:16

Laying down your life for someone is a sign of your great love for him. I remember a Christian sister who had a great ministry and several open doors for serving God ahead of her. One day, she fell in love with a man from her hometown, who was already married. Because of her great love for this man, she sacrificed her ministry, she sacrificed her pastor, she sacrificed her children, she sacrificed her husband, she sacrificed her spiritual father, she sacrificed her parents and she sacrificed her closeness to the brethren for this man.

Indeed, she gave up everything so that she could have the love of this man. It is the great sacrifices she made that revealed how much she loved this man. Hereby we perceive love: when someone lays down his life for it.

If you love the Lord, you will lay down your life for the brethren. What do you do for the church? What do you do for Christians? What do you do for people who are washed by the blood of Jesus? Everyone makes sacrifices for one reason or another. If you love the Lord, you will make sacrifices for your brothers and sisters in Christ. You will lay down your life for the brethren. Laying down your life for the brethren is a great sign of loving the Lord.

3. **If you love the Lord, you will have compassion for the brethren.**

But whoso hath this world's good, and seeth his brother have need, and shutteth up his bowels of COMPASSION FROM HIM, HOW DWELLETH THE LOVE OF GOD IN HIM?

1 John 3: 17

Jesus said unto him, If thou wilt be perfect, go and sell that thou hast, and give to the poor, and thou shalt have treasure in heaven: and come and follow me.

Matthew 19:21

Having compassion for people who have problems is a sign of your love for the Lord. It is indeed a sign of your closeness to the Lord. A lot of people have problems and needs. As you grow in your love for God, you will start feeling what God feels for these people.

As you get closer to someone, you start to find out his needs, his desires, his preferences and his wishes. Your understanding of a person's needs, desires, wishes are a revelation of your closeness to the person. The closer you are to someone, the closer you will be to his real problems.

One day, some people bought a present for me. Although they had made a great effort, their choice of a gift was out of order. It was not something I wanted or desired. It was not something I could even use. It was not something I liked. It was not something that I had wished for. They had completely misread me. This misplaced and misdirected gift revealed that they were not as close to me as they thought. They were not close to my mind. They were not close to my heart and that is why they bought this unusable gift for me.

When we are close to the Lord, we will understand his heart. When we love the Lord we will feel what he feels and be close to His deepest desires.

One of God's deepest feelings is His feeling for lost and suffering humanity. Jesus said, "I was hungry. I was thirsty. I was naked. I was sick. I was in prison." Jesus spoke of these terrible human conditions and stirred us up to care for them. He said that all those who show compassion would be blessed.

4. If you love the Lord, you will be a shepherd so that you can care for the brethren.

So when they had dined, Jesus saith to Simon Peter, Simon, son of Jonas, lovest thou me more than these? He saith unto him, Yea, Lord; thou knowest that I love thee. He saith unto him, feed my lambs. He saith to him again the second time, Simon, son of Jonas, lovest thou me? He saith unto him, Yea, Lord; thou knowest that I love thee. He saith unto him, feed my sheep. He saith unto him the third time, Simon, son of Jonas, lovest thou me? Peter was grieved because he said unto him the third time, Lovest thou me? And he said unto him, Lord, thou knowest all things; thou knowest that I love thee. Jesus saith unto him, feed my sheep.

John 21:15-17

Jesus asked Peter if he loved Him. If you love me, feed my sheep. Feeding the sheep and looking after them is one of the greatest signs that you love God. Jesus spoke to Peter and said, "Feed my sheep if you love me."

Pastoring people and teaching them the word of God is a sign that you love Jesus. Every pastor is a God-lover. I encourage you to be a pastor, a carer and a feeder of the sheep. God looks on lovingly when you teach and feed the people of God. It is nice that you give offerings and that you pay tithes. But Jesus did not say, "If you love me, pay your tithes." Jesus did not say, "If you love me, give a lot of offerings." Jesus did not say, "If you love me, be a member of the Building committee." Jesus did not say, "If you love me, join the Business Community."

Jesus was clear on what Peter had to do if he loved the Lord; Feed my sheep! Teach my people! Tend my lambs! This instruction is a great and clear revelation of what to do if you love Jesus. If you love the Lord, you will feed, you will gather, you will carry and you will lead the brethren to God. Feeding, gathering, carrying and leading God's people are a great sign of your loving God.

He shall FEED his flock like a shepherd: he shall GATHER the lambs with his arm, and CARRY them in his bosom, and shall gently LEAD those that are with young.

Isaiah 40:11

20

CHAPTER 4

If You Love the Lord: You Will Love His House

HOW AMIABLE ARE THY TABERNACLES, O Lord of hosts! My soul longeth, yea, even fainteth for the courts of the Lord: my heart and my flesh crieth out for the living God.

Psalm 84:1-2

1. If you love the Lord, you will love His house.

Lord, I HAVE LOVED THE HABITATION OF THY HOUSE, and the place where thine honour dwelleth.

Psalm 26:8

Those who love God love His house! David said clearly, "I love the habitation of your house." The NIV says it even more clearly: "LORD, I love the house where you live, the place where your glory dwells" (Psalm 26:8, NIV). Loving the house of God is a sure sign that you love the Lord.

2. If you love the Lord, you will spend a lot of time in His house.

For a day in thy courts is better than a thousand. I had rather be a doorkeeper in the house of my God, than to dwell in the tents of wickedness.

Psalm 84:10

If you love the Lord, you will spend a lot of time in His house. If you love the Lord, you will love spending the whole day in His presence. No amount of time will be too long to spend in church. It is because you do not love the Lord that you find church services long. It is because you do not love the Lord that you can watch a series on television for hours and hours. It is the television series and the movies that you love! If you love the Lord, you will prefer to be in His house than to be anywhere else.

3. If you love the Lord, you will build His house.

Moreover, because I have set my affection to the house of my God, I have of mine own proper good, of gold and silver, which I have given to the house of my God, over and above all that I have prepared for the holy house,

1 Chronicles 29:3

King David did everything in his power to build the church. If you love the Lord, you will build His house. If you love the Lord, you will give so that His house can be built. If you love the Lord, you will help missionaries who are trying to build His house. If you love the Lord, you will support any effort to build the church. If you love the Lord, you will do the work of a shepherd to help to build up the congregation. Building up the congregation is building the house of God. Lovers of God are always lovers of his house. Lovers of God are always builders of His house.

4. If you love the Lord, you will fight for His house.

Jesus loved the house of God. Everyone who loves God will love His house. Your love for something is revealed by your responses to it. Your reaction to someone being violated reveals how much you love the person. Jesus' reaction to His Father's house being violated revealed how much He loved His father's house. Wicked businessmen, moneychangers and money launderers had filled the temple. Jesus made a scourge of small cords and drove them out. The reaction of Jesus to the violation of His father's house revealed His love for God. Anyone who loves God will love the house of God and will fight for it.

> And found in the temple those that sold oxen and sheep and doves, and the changers of money sitting: And when he had made a scourge of small cords, he drove them all out of the temple, and the sheep, and the oxen; and poured out the changers' money, and overthrew the tables; And said unto them that sold doves, Take these things hence; make not my Father's house an house of merchandise. And his disciples remembered that it was written, the zeal of thine house hath eaten me up.
>
> John 2:14-17

5. If you love the Lord, you will see the beauty of God in His house.

> One thing have I desired of the Lord, that will I seek after; that I may dwell in the house of the Lord all the days of my life, TO BEHOLD THE BEAUTY OF THE LORD, AND TO ENQUIRE IN HIS TEMPLE. For in the time of trouble he shall hide me in his pavilion: in the secret of

his tabernacle shall he hide me; he shall set me up upon a rock.

Psalm 27:4-5

If you love the Lord, you will see His greatness when you go to His house. If you love someone, you will see the good things of the person. If you love someone, you will see good things only. If you hate someone, you will see bad things only.

Those who hate me see all my faults. Those who dislike me find something wrong with my preaching, my teaching and my ministry. The pastors under me, who love me, are filled with eyes of admiration. My mockers and scoffers see many things I do as negative and as evil. It is amazing! If you love someone, he cannot go wrong. When you love someone, everything about him is beautiful.

The beauty of the Lord is what is seen when God-lovers go to His temple. Those who have eyes to see, see the beauty of God. You will notice more nice things about God, as you love Him more.

6. If you love the Lord, you will be glad when they say, "Let us go to the house of God."

I was glad when they said unto me, Let us go into the house of the Lord. Our feet shall stand within thy gates, O Jerusalem. Jerusalem is builded as a city that is compact together: Whither the tribes go up, the tribes of the Lord, unto the testimony of Israel, to give thanks unto the name of the Lord. For there are set thrones of judgment, the thrones of the house of David. Pray for the peace of Jerusalem: they shall prosper that love thee.

Psalm 122:1-6

Your attitude towards the house of God reveals your love for God. Some people react negatively when there is a suggestion to have fish for lunch. Some people react negatively when there is a suggestion to go swimming.

Some married people react negatively when there is a suggestion to have sex. What do these negative reactions reveal? These hesitant reactions reveal unwillingness, reluctance and a disinclination. They reveal that you do not love what is being suggested.

You are always glad when what you love is suggested! If you love doing something, you will be glad when there is a suggestion to do it. If you love the Lord, you will be glad when they say, "Let us go to the house of the Lord."

7. **If you love the Lord, you will consider it a favour to go to the house of God.**

    And the king said unto Zadok, Carry back the ark of God into the city: if I shall find favour in the eyes of the LORD, he will bring me again, and shew me both it, and his habitation:

    2 Samuel 15:25

    When you love the house of God, you will consider it such an honour to go to the house of God. David felt that God was favouring him when he allowed him to go to church. Some people consider it a great privilege when they have a chance to go for a holiday in the Bahamas. Others consider it a great honour if they have a chance to go on a cruise. Yet still, there are those who consider it a special honour to have the chance to go shopping in Paris. King David considered it a great honour if he had a chance to go to the house of God.

8. **If you love the Lord, you will have strong feelings about church.**

    How amiable are thy tabernacles, O LORD of hosts! My soul longeth, yea, even fainteth for the courts of the LORD: my heart and my flesh crieth out for the living God.

    Psalm 84:1-2

Strong feelings are a sign of love! David described very strong feelings for the house of God. David said he was fainting because of the house of God. He described how his heart and his flesh were both crying out for the living God. These strong feelings for the house of God are the greatest evidence of your love. Your great love for anything is evidenced by the strong feelings you have for it.

9. If you love the Lord, anyone searching for you will find you in the house of God.

And it came to pass, that after three days they found him in the temple, sitting in the midst of the doctors, both hearing them, and asking them questions.

Luke 2:46

If you love the Lord, you will be found in the house of God. Your love drives you to the place where your lover is.

One day, a married man fell in love with a beautiful young girl. He began to have an affair with this lady. One day, whilst in the car with his wife, he drove straight to his girlfriend's house. He had no intentions of going there. He was so used to going there. Without even understanding why, he drove to his girlfriend's house with his wife sitting by him. He was completely programmed to go to the house where his lover was.

Indeed, you will always go to the house where the one you love lives!

Jesus Christ was lost. His parents could not find Him. For three days they searched and searched. They checked in all the fish and chips bars looking for Jesus but He was not there. They checked in his school friend's house but He was not there. They checked other carpentry shops and businesses in the area but Jesus was not there. Eventually, they found Jesus Christ in the church. His parents were not happy with Him. But He simply pointed out to them that there was only one place that He could possibly be in his spare time, and that was church. If you love

26

the Lord, you will be found in the church. When they search for you, they will find you in the house of God.

CHAPTER 5

If You Love the Lord: You Will Have Feelings for Him

I remember how eager you were to please me as a young bride long ago, how you loved me and followed me even through the barren wilderness.

Jeremiah 2:2 NLT

1. If you love the Lord, you will go after Him. You will be kind to Him.

> Moreover the word of the Lord came to me, saying, Go and cry in the ears of Jerusalem, saying, Thus saith the Lord; I remember thee, THE KINDNESS OF THY YOUTH, THE LOVE OF THINE ESPOUSALS, when THOU WENTEST AFTER ME IN THE WILDERNESS, in a land that was not sown. Israel was holiness unto the Lord, and the firstfruits of his increase: all that devour him shall offend; evil shall come upon them, saith the Lord. Hear ye the word of the Lord, O house of Jacob, and all the families of the house of Israel: Thus saith the Lord, What iniquity have your fathers found in me, that they are gone far from me, and have walked after vanity, and are become vain? Neither said they, Where is the Lord that brought us up out of the land of Egypt, that led us through the wilderness, through a land of deserts and of pits, through a land of drought, and of the shadow of death, through a land that no man passed through, and where no man dwelt? And I brought you into a plentiful country, to eat the fruit thereof and the goodness thereof; but when ye entered, ye defiled my land, and made mine heritage an abomination.

Jeremiah 2:1-7

If you love the Lord, you will have feelings for Him. Love without feelings and without passion is not good love. There are people who are flat and expressionless. It is not easy to love people who do not show any feelings or passion. Unfortunately, this is the lot of some married people. Some people are simply unemotional and bland.

Although it seems like a minor thing, experiencing love without feelings is a difficult thing. Being married to someone who is undemonstrative and unexciting may seem like a trivial problem, it is not. It is a tragedy of enormous proportion. Indeed, one definition of a dragon is "a strict and watchful woman".

Who would like to be married to a strict and watchful person who, instead of showing desire, pleasure and happiness, has turned into a strict and watchful overseer? That is what it means to be married to a dragon!

God said, "I remember your kindness and I remember the love of thy espousals." This is a loaded statement. Only an experienced person would know that a lot of couples have ceased to experience kindness in marriage. Many couples have ceased from "the love of thy espousals." Read it carefully from the Living Bible: "Go and shout this message to Jerusalem. This is what the LORD says: "I remember how eager you were to please me as a young bride long ago, how you loved me and followed me even through the barren wilderness." (Jeremiah 2:2, NLT)

If you love the Lord, you will be like a young bride who is eager to please God. If you love the Lord, you will follow him anywhere. If you love the Lord, you will be filled with attention and devotion. If you love the Lord, you will be like a newlyweds. If you love the Lord, there will be feelings, there will be passion, there will be joy, there will be sounds, there will be noise, there will be jumping and there will be dancing. There will be excitement! There will be smiles! There will be laughter! It is time to love the Lord with feelings!

Dignity is not a fruit of the Holy Spirit. Joy is a fruit of the Holy Spirit. It is better to have joy than to have dignity. The joy of the Lord is your strength. The joy of the Lord is a source of strength for you. The joy of the Lord is not your weakness. The fact that you are joyful and passionate does not make you weaker, it makes you stronger!

2. If you love the Lord, you will rise and seek Him.

BY NIGHT ON MY BED I SOUGHT HIM WHOM MY SOUL LOVETH: I sought him, but I found him not. I will rise now, and go about the city in the streets, and in the broad ways I will seek him whom my soul loveth: I sought him, but I found him not. The watchmen that go about the city found me: to whom I said, Saw ye him whom my soul loveth? It was but a little that I passed from them, but I found him whom my soul loveth: I held him, and would not let him go, until I had brought him into my mother's house, and into the chamber of her that conceived me.

Song of Songs 3:1-4

By night, I sought him whom my soul loveth!

You will always go seeking after the one you love.

If you love the Lord, you will go after Him. Love is often assessed by who started it all and who went after whom. If you seek someone, if you follow someone, if you pursue someone, it is assumed that you have great love for the person. If you pursue someone, it is assumed that you are the one with the passion, the feelings and the desire.

When people have an illegitimate affair, there is usually an argument afterward about who went after whom. "You started it! You came after me! You pursued me! You hunted me down! You initiated it several times!" These are the common accusations and counteraccusations from those who have fallen in and out of love.

Married couples have fallen out of love when they do not initiate love games.

"I am there". "I am available." "I never say no." These are common statements from couples that are no longer in love. I may not initiate love but I am available if he wants to do anything! Surely, these are statements that come from those who are past loving! There is no seeking of anyone by anyone! There is no more love!

By night, I sought him whom my soul loveth!

God also assesses love by who seeks whom!

Do you seek God? Do you initiate love? Do you start the relationship with God?

Do you find time to wait on Him? Do you go away and spend time in His presence?

Spending a lot of time praying prayers that have been organised by your church is not the same as you going on your own to seek the Lord.

I sought him whom my soul loveth! You will always go seeking after the one you love!

CHAPTER 6

If You Love the Lord:
You Will Give Something

For God so loved the world, that he gave his only begotten Son, that whosoever believeth in him should not perish, but have everlasting life. For God sent not his Son into the world to condemn the world; but that the world through him might be saved.

John 3:16-17

Giving has always been the greatest sign of love. God loved the world so much that He gave His only begotten Son. Love is like oil. You cannot just give oil to somebody. You have to put it into something in order to give it to him. There will always be what you are giving to prove your love and your sincerity. Without a bottle you will not be able to make a gift of oil to someone.

Without having something to give, you are often unable to show love. Watch out for people who just talk a lot and make a lot of promises. You must be wary of speeches. You must be wary of people who talk a lot but have little to show for their love.

I have met many kinds of people who have various levels of love. Rest assured that those who speak a lot but act little are not the ones who really love you.

One day, I met a man who spoke so much about my life and how he could help me. He seemed willing and eager to help me in any way possible. He showed me a business that I could engage in. He spoke a lot and offered a lot of advice based on his own experience. Then he took me in a car to a nearby town and showed me something that had a great potential to help me in the business. By the evening, I was exhausted, but excited at the great potential of my new business.

All through the day I had been thinking to myself that this kind man would be the best person to help me financially. He had shown so much interest and been with me the whole day. I knew that God had brought him specially to help me. When I asked him for financial help to start the business, which he had proposed and taught me about, he immediately backed off. "So sorry," he said. He would not be able to help me at all!

This man was not a poor person. Indeed, I knew people that he had recently given gifts of over ten thousand pounds sterling to. Indeed, he was a living millionaire whom I had encountered. This man's love for me did not extend beyond his words. He did not give even give one dollar towards the business. There are many people whose love does not extend beyond their words.

God's love extends beyond words. God's love is backed with real actions. God's love is backed with giving. If you love you will give! God so loved that He gave.

There are people who say big things but do little. That is why some people are called Mr. Dolittle. There are people who may shout out and say, "My son! My daughter!" they introduce you all over the place as a son to them. In reality, they have done very little to prove that you are a son or a daughter.

One day, an elderly man was introduced to a visitor by his son-in-law. When the visitor left, the father-in-law called the son-in-law and told him, "I do not like it when you refer to me as your father-in-law. I am your father. You are my son. I am not your father-in-law. I am your father! Wow. The son-in-law was greatly touched by this show of love. From that time, the elderly man repeated this declaration many times. You are my son. You are not my son-in-law. I am your father. I am not your father-in-law. The years passed by and one day this elderly man died. There was a big funeral and this elderly man was buried by all his sons, daughters, sons-in-law and daughters in law.

The son-in-law who had been told that he was a son and not a son-in-law was expectant that he would be treated as a son and not as a son-in-law. However, he noticed at the funeral that the sons were separated from the sons-in-law. This was the first sign to him that perhaps the sonship was not as real as he hoped.

But he kept hope alive till the day this rich man's will was read. The will was so long because it contained the details of so much wealth that was being distributed to the children. Unfortunately, the son-in-laws name was not in the will. This young man was devastated because he had believed that he had actually become one of the sons.

Indeed his father-in-law's love for him did not go beyond words. It was the love of words. It was love without giving. If you love, you will give. God did not just love us by speaking His Word from Heaven. He gave us His Son to prove the reality of His love. Loving always includes giving.

Watch out for those who claim to love you. What do they give you to prove their love for you? Is it just words? Think about all the boyfriends you had. What did they give you? And what did you give them? You gave yourself to them, and they gave you nothing!

Think about the man who married you. He gave you his name. He gave you his ring. He gave you his commitment. He gave you his life. He gave you a beautiful wedding. He gave you the status and the social standing. What do you give him in return? Think of all the acrobatics and gymnastics you did for those boys who didn't love you. Why wouldn't you give more to the one who gave you his life in marriage? Amazingly, people give little or nothing in return to the one who loved them.

There are several things you can give to prove your love for God.

Seven Things You Can Give to Prove Your Love

1. If you love the Lord, you will give your money.

But since you excel in everything—in faith, in speech, in knowledge, in complete earnestness and in the love we have kindled in you—see that you also excel in this GRACE OF GIVING. I am not commanding you, but I want to TEST THE SINCERITY OF YOUR LOVE by comparing it with the earnestness of others.

2 Corinthians 8:7-8 (NIV)

Giving your money is a sign of loving someone. The Corinthians' proof of love was demonstrated in their ability to give and to support. The grace of giving reveals the grace to love. Selfish people are loveless people. Self-centred people have no love to give. People who constantly think about themselves, what they can get, what they can gain, are loveless people. It is not nice to experience loveless people. Loveless people stir up rejection and hatred.

People without love have nothing to give. They are constantly looking for what is going to be given to them. They are constantly expecting someone to buy something for them or to give something to them. They exist to receive things! This is why loveless people are often rejected. After a while, the self-centredness and the selfishness are easy to see and they are rejected.

2. **If you love the Lord, you will give your loyalties. Ruth showed her love by giving her commitment to her mother-in-law.**

And he shall be unto thee a restorer of thy life, and a nourisher of thine old age: FOR THY DAUGHTER IN LAW, WHICH LOVETH THEE, which is better to thee than seven sons, hath born him.

Ruth 4:15

The lesson of Ruth is a lesson of love. Ruth loved her mother-in-law. She gave her commitment and loyalty to her mother-in-law. She said, "Intreat me not to leave thee, or to return from following after thee: for whither thou goest, I will go; and where thou lodgest, I will lodge: thy people shall be my people, and thy God my God: Where thou diest, will I die, and there will I be buried: the LORD do so to me, and more also, if ought but death part thee and me" (Ruth 1:16-17).

These are famous words that have been quoted and re-quoted through the centuries. The loyalty, the love, the commitment, the fidelity, the pledge, the assurances, the promises and the vows of Ruth are basically expressions of love. This is why people say that the daughter-in-law who loves you is worth more than seven sons. Loving God is worth more than anything else. It is the greatest commandment. If you love the Lord, you will give him your vows, your commitment, your loyalties and your promises. You will keep your promises because you love the Lord. You are worth more than seven other Christians when you love the Lord.

3. If you love the Lord, you will give your life.

For God so loved the world, that he gave his only begotten Son, that whosoever believeth in him should not perish, but have everlasting life. For God sent not his Son into the world to condemn the world; but that the world through him might be saved.

John 3:16-17

Do you wonder why God wants your life? Because He gave his life! Jesus gave everything to have you. But you would not give up your foolish boyfriends and girlfriends for Jesus. You would not give yourself when you were beautiful. When you were fresh and beautiful you gave yourself to other men, other girls and other evils. God wants the choice parts of your life too.

If you love the Lord, you will not wait until you are old and frail before you give yourself to God. If you love the Lord, you will give your best life to Him!

There are many people who want to give God some evenings of their life.

O Lord, you can have 7.00 pm to 9.00 pm on Tuesdays and Thursdays!

O Lord, you can have 8.00 am to 10.00 am on Sundays!

O Lord, you can have my life now; I'm over sixty-five years!

O Lord, the bank doesn't want me, the hospital doesn't want me, the school doesn't want me, and the pharmacy shop does not want me. No one wants me!

Here am I Lord, you can have your way with my life! Take my grey hairs. Take my waning strength! Take my fading beauty! Take my wrinkled face! Take my discoloured skin! Take my potbelly! Take my sagging stomach! Take my tiredness! Take my bad attitude! Take my poor health and use it. If you can use anything, Lord, you can use me now!

4. If you love the Lord, you will give your time.

And if thy brother, an Hebrew man, or an Hebrew woman, be sold unto thee, and serve thee six years; then in the seventh year thou shalt let him go free from thee. And when thou sendest him out free from thee, thou shalt not let him go away empty: Thou shalt furnish him liberally out of thy flock, and out of thy floor, and out of thy winepress: of that wherewith the LORD thy God hath blessed thee thou shalt give unto him.

And thou shalt remember that thou wast a bondman in the land of Egypt, and the LORD thy God redeemed thee: therefore I command thee this thing to day.

And it shall be, if he say unto thee, I will not go away from thee; because he loveth thee and thine house, because he is well with thee;

Deuteronomy 15:12-16

In this scripture, we see the servant deciding to stay with his master. That is truly a sign of love. The servant decided to give the rest of his life to live in the presence of his master.

Staying with someone is a decision to give your time and your presence. There are people who have a chance to be near you but they take every opportunity to leave your presence. They move to the back when they could be in the front.

Some married women serve their husbands food but without much love. They would dump the food in front of the husband and go away from his presence. The more loving wives would serve the food and sit by their husbands as they ate. In this way, they give the food as well as their time and their presence.

Why not serve food with love rather than food without love? As the scripture says, it is better to have dinner with love than dinner without love.

Better is a DINNER of herbs WHERE LOVE IS, than a stalled ox and hatred therewith

Proverbs 15:17

God wants you to serve with love! God wants you to preach the word of God with love.

5. If you love the Lord, you will give a church building.

And a certain centurion's servant, who was dear unto him, was sick, and ready to die. And when he heard of Jesus, he sent unto him the elders of the Jews, beseeching him that he would come and heal his servant. And when they came to Jesus, they besought him instantly, saying, that he was worthy for whom he should do this: For he loveth our nation, and he hath built us a synagogue.

Luke 7:2-5

The centurion was considered worthy of a miracle because he had built a whole synagogue. If someone gives a whole house to you, he must love you very much. The centurion's love for Israel had caused him to build a whole synagogue. Today, there are many people who love God so much that they are building entire church buildings by themselves. Your ability to build a whole church reveals your love for God. Do not let anything hold you back from building a church before you die. If someone gives a whole house to you, he must love you very much. When you give a whole building to God, it is a sign that you love him very much!

6. If you love the Lord, you will give this world's good.

Hereby perceive we the love of God, because he laid down his life for us: and we ought to lay down our lives for the brethren.

1 John 3:16

If you love the Lord you will give this world's good. Whatever good thing there is in the world, it is time to give it to God. You can give God more than money. You can present the Lord with the fruits of your field. You can love God by presenting your tomatoes, your car, your furniture and anything you possess.

7. If you love the Lord, you will give everything.

The Father loveth the Son, and hath given all things into his hand.

John 3:35

When you love someone, you will give everything you have. The father loved the son so much that he gave everything. It is time to love God so much that you give everything. God has given all things into the hands of Jesus because he loves the Son. The Father gave all things to the Son because the Son gave all things to the Father!

CHAPTER 7

If You Love the Lord: You Will Love His Word

CONSIDER HOW I LOVE THY PRECEPTS: quicken me, O LORD, according to thy lovingkindness.

Thy word is true from the beginning: and every one of thy righteous judgments endureth for ever.

Princes have persecuted me without a cause: but MY HEART STANDETH IN AWE OF THY WORD.

I REJOICE AT THY WORD, as one that findeth great spoil.

I hate and abhor lying: but THY LAW DO I LOVE.

Seven times a day do I praise thee because of thy righteous judgments.

GREAT PEACE HAVE THEY WHICH LOVE THY LAW: and nothing shall offend them.

LORD, I have hoped for thy salvation, and done thy commandments.

My soul hath kept thy testimonies; and I LOVE THEM EXCEEDINGLY.

I have kept thy precepts and thy testimonies: for all my ways are before thee.

Psalm 119:159-168

Ten Laws for Loving the Word

1. We shall consider how much you love the word of God. "Consider how I love thy precepts: quicken me, O Lord, according to thy lovingkindness" (Psalm 119:159)

2. Your Word is true from the beginning till the end. "Thy word is true from the beginning: and every one of thy righteous judgments endureth for ever" (Psalm 119:160)

3. Your heart must stand in awe at the greatness of the word of God. "Princes have persecuted me without a cause: but my heart standeth in awe of thy word" (Psalm 119:161)

4. You must rejoice at the word of God. "I rejoice at thy word, as one that findeth great spoil" (Psalm 119:162)

5. You must hate lying and love the truth of God's Word. "I hate and abhor lying: but thy law do I love" (Psalm 119:163)

6. You must praise God seven times a day because of His righteous Word. "Seven times a day do I praise thee because of thy righteous judgments" (Psalm 119:164)

7. You must love the law and it will give you great peace. "Great peace have they which love thy law: and nothing shall offend them" (Psalm 119:165)

8. You must hope for salvation through the word of God. "Lord, I have hoped for thy salvation, and done thy commandments" (Psalm 119:166)

9. You must love the testimonies of God exceedingly. "My soul hath kept thy testimonies; and I love them exceedingly" (Psalm 119:167)

10. You must keep and obey the precepts and testimonies that you have fallen in love with. "I have kept thy precepts and thy testimonies: for all my ways are before thee" (Psalm 119:168)

If you love the Lord you will love His Word. The passage above reveals a person who has fallen in love with the word of God. Loving God is the same as loving his Word. In the beginning was the Word. The Word was with God. The Word was God. God is His Word!

If you love God it means you love the Word. If you love the Word it means you love God.

In the beginning was the Word, and the Word was with God, and THE WORD WAS GOD. The same was in the beginning with God.

John 1:1-2

I can often tell when people love me by the love they have for the Word that I have preached or shared. A person is identified by his words. If you love the words and the instructions of a person, you usually have a good relationship with him. If you say something to someone and the person misunderstands you, it is often a sign of a difficult and poor relationship.

I once spoke to someone and he got angry. He became rebellious and left the church. He said many negative things about me. Obviously, he did not love my words to him and he also did not love me.

You can tell when people love God. They love to listen to his word. They love going to church. They love listening to sermons. They love to hear the preaching of the Word. They love to read the Word. They love to study the Word. They love to memorize the Word. They love to sing the Word.

Once I decided to monitor a backslidden sister's Christian life. I wanted to find out if she was growing in her relationship with God. This Christian sister decided to trick me into thinking that she had returned from her backsliding and that she was now serving the Lord properly. She would attend church and make sure I saw that she was present. Sometimes, she would come and sit near the front intentionally, so that I would notice. There are times she would come to church for a few minutes and then disappear. Her appearances in the church services to "mark the register" were completely misleading.

She thought that she could deceive me into thinking that she was now a serious Christian. But I knew that she was not serious in the Lord. I knew that it was all a cover-up and I had decided to use something else to monitor her Christian life. I decided to use her love for the Word as the best indicator of her spiritual state. I found out secretly that she never read her Bible. I found out that she had no idea about what was really being preached in church because she never really listened. I decided to use her love for the word of God as my indicator. Even though she attended church, I found out that she never listened to the messages. She never listened to the podcast.

Your love for the Word of God reveals your love for God. If you love God you will love His Word! You will love the preaching of the Word. You will love the sound of the Word. You will love those who preach the Word because they carry and deliver what you really love.

CONSIDER HOW I LOVE THY PRECEPTS: quicken me, O LORD, according to thy lovingkindness.
Psalm 119:159

It is time to consider how a person loves the Word. The way you love the Word reveals how you love God. You must always consider how much a person loves the Word.

Loving the Lord includes loving the hard parts of His Word. There are nice parts of the word of God. There are prophecies that predict nice things to us. There are promises of greatness, of victory and of salvation. There are scriptures that sound too good to be true. These ones are easy to love. At that point people shout "Amen", "Hallelujah" and jump to their feet. I can assure you that there is a lot in the word of God that will make you shout and scream, "I receive it!"

All scripture is given by inspiration of God, and is profitable for doctrine, for reproof, for correction, for instruction in righteousness:

2 Timothy 3:16

1. If you love the Lord, you will love the doctrine of His Word.

2. If you love the Lord, you will love the rebukes of His Word.

3. If you love the Lord, you will love the reproofs of His Word.

4. If you love the Lord, you will love the correction of His Word.

5. If you love the Lord, you will love the instructions of His Word.

Perhaps, the greatest revelation of your character is your ability to receive the hard parts of the word of God. As the years go by, you will find out that the harder parts are probably more important than the nice and easy prophecies of good things.

Many prophets have learned to prophesy good things. People want to hear good things! It is called "itching ears". People have "itching ears" and will encourage you to scratch their ears so that they hear exactly what they want to hear.

If you were fed on a diet of lollipops, sweets, sugar and honey, you would not be healthy. They may be nice for the moment but with time you will find yourself going to the dentist all the time and you will develop obesity and other health problems. You may have been angry with your mother for insisting that you eat vegetables and other healthier foods. Your mother only wanted you to grow up strong and healthy. But you were angry with her for giving you okro, spinach, carrots and cabbage.

Make sure you love every aspect of the Word so that you can grow up healthy and strong in Jesus.

CHAPTER 8

If You Love the Lord: You Will Love His Messengers

For the Father himself loveth you, because ye have loved me, and have believed that I came out from God.

John 16:27

I f you love the Lord, you will love the one whom the Lord sends. You will love Jesus and you will love His messengers.

When you love someone, you love the person's wife, children and family. Indeed, anything that is close to someone you love represents the person. That is why when the enemy wants to attack you, he may attack someone you love.

Satan understands the principle of representation. Whoever represents you is you! Jesus said, "He who receives you receives me."

Anyone who welcomes you welcomes me, and anyone who welcomes me welcomes the one who sent me.

Matthew 10:40, (NIV)

Your attitude towards God's messengers reveals your love for God. A real God-lover is very tender and soft towards God's messengers. As soon as a God-lover hears that a servant of God is at his door, his attitude will be welcoming and loving. His welcoming attitude reveals his love for God.

Whatever you do to the messenger of God reveals your attitude towards God Himself. People who hate God hate God's messengers also. It is easy to see the God-haters on social media.

Those who have no respect for God's servants have no respect for God. There are many people who insult God's servants. They do not realise that each time they do this they demote themselves further.

Watch out for your attitude towards God's servants. No matter the denomination they belong to, you must treat God's servants with utmost respect, love and care. The love and care you show for God's servant reveals the tenderness, love and affection you have for Almighty God Himself.

Do not ever claim that you love God when you do not love His servants.

CHAPTER 9

If You Love the Lord: You Will Marry Him

Go and cry in the ears of Jerusalem, saying, Thus saith the LORD; I remember thee, the kindness of thy youth, the love of thine espousals, when thou wentest after me in the wilderness, in a land that was not sown.

Jeremiah 2:2

For the husband is the head of the wife, even as Christ is the head of the church: and he is the saviour of the body. Therefore as the church is subject unto Christ, so let the wives be to their own husbands in every thing. Husbands, love your wives, even as Christ also loved the church, and gave himself for it; That he might sanctify and cleanse it with the washing of water by the word, That he might present it to himself a glorious church, not having spot, or wrinkle, or any such thing; but that it should be holy and without blemish. So ought men to love their wives as their own bodies. He that loveth his wife loveth himself. For no man ever yet hated his own flesh; but nourisheth and cherisheth it, even as the Lord the church: For we are members of his body, of his flesh, and of his bones. For this cause shall a man leave his father and mother, and shall be joined unto his wife, and they two shall be one flesh. This is a great mystery: but I speak concerning Christ and the church.

Ephesians 5:23-32

he church is clearly expected to have a love affair with the Lord. He is the head and we are the body. The mystery of marriage is the mystery of Christ and the church. All through the Bible, we see God referring to himself as our Lover. His relationship with Israel is always described as a love affair that went sour. In the scripture below, the prophet informs Israel that God is their husband.

> For thy Maker is thine husband; the Lord of hosts is his name; and thy Redeemer the Holy One of Israel; The God of the whole earth shall he be called. For the Lord hath called thee as a woman forsaken and grieved in spirit, and a wife of youth, when thou wast refused, saith thy God. For a small moment have I forsaken thee; but with great mercies will I gather thee. In a little wrath I hid my face from thee for a moment; but with everlasting kindness will I have mercy on thee, saith the Lord thy Redeemer.

Isaiah 54:5-8

It is time to accept this reality and flow as the bride of Jesus Christ. God wants us to flow with him as though we are married to Him. God will not be satisfied with any other kind of love relationship. He wants a marital love relationship with you.

Seven Signs that You Are Married to Christ

1. You are married to Christ when you feel a lot of love for the Lord. You must feel a lot of love for Jesus. You must feel a lot of love for the Father. You must feel a lot of love for the Holy Spirit.

2. You are married to Christ when your relationship with the Lord exists to the exclusion of all others. Marriage is a relationship that exists to the exclusion of all others. The powerful presence of any other person will surely interfere with the love relationship between you and the Lord. Christians who are obsessed with having good family lives and are excessively concerned with claims that marriage and

children are more important than serving God, are usually unable to achieve a strong marriage relationship with the Lord. You can develop a relationship with the Lord to the exclusion of all others.

3. You are married to Christ when there is a lifelong commitment. When you are married to the Lord, there is no question about leaving Him. There is no uncertainty about how long and how far the relationship will go. Marriage relationships are forever.

4. You are married to Christ when there is a lot of conversation between you and the Lord. Continuous talking and chatting is the hallmark of every good marital relationship. When Christians fall in love with God, there is continuous talking and chatting with Him. There will be prayer and more prayer. There will be intercession. There will be giving of thanks. There will be supplications. There will be praises. There will be worship. These kinds of conversations will go on endlessly because there is great love for the Lord.

5. You are married to Christ when you delight in Him and you are excited to be with him. You must desire the Lord and be excited to be with Him and to see Him.

6. You are married to Christ when you are in His presence most of the time. Married couples are together most of the time, in theory. Staying in the presence of someone is a sign that you are married to the person. If you are a visitor, you have to leave after a couple of hours.

7. You are married to Christ when your relationship with the Lord brings forth fruits. Married couples bring forth fruit. They have children. Your strong relationship with the Lord will cause fruits to come forth. It is only a deep marital relationship with the Lord that results in much fruit with Jesus.

CHAPTER 10

If You Love the Lord: Keep Only One Master

Wherefore shew ye to them, and before the churches, the proof of your love, and of our boasting on your behalf.

2 Corinthians 8:24

No servant can serve two masters: for either he will hate the one, and love the other; or else he will hold to the one, and despise the other. Ye cannot serve God and mammon.

Luke 16:13

There are many people that claim to love someone. Why do people claim to love someone? Sometimes, people claim to love someone because they want to convince the person to marry them or to give them some favour. "O, I love you," they will say. But really, they do not!

When a man has loved several other girls, he may have a tough time proving to the next girl that he does love her.

When a girl has loved several other boys, she may have a tough time proving to the next boy that she does love him.

Research has shown that relationships, which experience unfaithfulness, are difficult to repair. Many times, such relationships can never be restored. Sometimes, people come back together for a season but give up after a while claiming they cannot handle the fact that their partner strayed into other relationships and expressed love, desire, commitment, interest, excitement and feelings to someone else.

Jesus was quite clear about this. You cannot love two masters. Jesus did not leave any grey areas. You cannot love two masters. There are many potential masters. There are many challengers for God's love. It is not easy to know what is in your heart. It is important to be aware of the possible challengers of your love for God.

1. **If you love the Lord, you will not love evil: You cannot love two masters.**

   And this is the condemnation, that light is come into the world, and MEN LOVED DARKNESS RATHER THAN LIGHT, because their deeds were evil. For every one that doeth evil hateth the light, neither cometh to the light, lest his deeds should be reproved. But he that doeth truth cometh to the light, that his deeds may be made manifest, that they are wrought in God.

   John 3:19-21

   Your love for darkness and your love for evil are proofs that you do not love the Lord. If you love the Lord you will flush out all other loves. Your love for darkness, secrets, shady things and mysteries, which create a departmentalized lifestyle, is evidence that you do not love God. Light has come into the world but darkness is what you prefer! Your love for the world, your love for evil, your love for wicked films, your love for pornography and your support for wicked men reveal that you do not love God.

Why boastest thou thyself in mischief, O mighty man? The goodness of God endureth continually. Thy tongue deviseth mischiefs; like a sharp razor, working deceitfully. THOU LOVEST EVIL MORE THAN GOOD; AND LYING RATHER THAN TO SPEAK RIGHTEOUSNESS. Selah. Thou lovest all devouring words, O thou deceitful tongue. God shall likewise destroy thee for ever, he shall take thee away, and pluck thee out of thy dwelling place, and root thee out of the land of the living. Selah.

Psalm 52:1-5

And I said, Hear, I pray you, O heads of Jacob, and ye princes of the house of Israel; is it not for you to know judgment? WHO HATE THE GOOD, AND LOVE THE EVIL; who pluck off their skin from off them, and their flesh from off their bones; who also eat the flesh of my people, and flay their skin from off them; and they break their bones, and chop them in pieces, as for the pot, and as flesh within the caldron. Then shall they cry unto the Lord, but he will not hear them: he will even hide his face from them at that time, as they have behaved themselves ill in their doings.

Micah 3:1-4

2. **If you love the Lord, you will not love strife: You cannot love two masters.**

HE LOVETH TRANSGRESSION THAT LOVETH STRIFE: and he that exalteth his gate seeketh destruction.

Proverbs 17:19

Your love for strife is proof that you do not love the Lord. Watch out for those who love quarrelling. Watch out for those who strive with you. Watch out for those who enjoy debating and arguing endlessly. Watch out for those who never have peace in their lives. Watch out for those who cannot live peaceably with others. Their love for strife is evidence that they do not love the Lord.

3. **If you love the Lord you will not love pleasure. You cannot love two masters.**

He that loveth pleasure shall be a poor man: he that loveth wine and oil shall not be rich.

Proverbs 21:17

Your love for pleasure is proof that you do not love the Lord. There are people who live for pleasure. There are those who need to have certain feelings at all costs. There are those who must enjoy the pleasures of sin, no matter what. Your love for these controlling pleasures reveals that you do not love the Lord.

4. **If you love the Lord, you will not love silver and gold: You cannot love two masters.**

When Jesus said you could not love two masters, He was referring to money as one of the two masters. Money and wealth are what men love. Men love money so much that they forsake the Almighty God. Indeed, he that loveth silver cannot also love the Lord. I have been in the ministry for some years. I have not seen anyone loving silver and loving God at the same time.

HE THAT LOVETH SILVER SHALL NOT BE SATISFIED WITH SILVER; NOR HE THAT LOVETH ABUNDANCE WITH INCREASE: THIS IS ALSO VANITY.

Ecclesiastes 5:10

Many ministers get to the place where they love gifts, money and wealth more than they love the Lord. Take a look at some of the great and well-known ministers of the gospel. Listen to their

56

preaching when they started out in ministry and when they were not following after rewards. You will notice a subtle change in the anointing.

"Thy princes (pastors) are rebellious, and companions of thieves: EVERY ONE LOVETH GIFTS, AND FOLLOWETH AFTER REWARDS: they judge not the fatherless, neither doth the cause of the widow come unto them" (Isaiah 1:23).

Money loving ministers with money-loving preaching with a money-loving emphasis will be a hallmark of the end time ministry. Just look around you. Just watch Christian television for five minutes and you will see the unmistakable sign of a fallen church with money-lovers instead of God-lovers in the pulpits. Anyone who loves money does not love the Lord. You cannot love two masters!

But mark this: There will be terrible times in the last days. People will be lovers of themselves, LOVERS OF MONEY, boastful, proud, abusive, disobedient to their parents, ungrateful, unholy, without love, unforgiving, slanderous, without self-control, brutal, not lovers of the good, treacherous, rash, conceited, lovers of pleasure rather than lovers of God

2 Timothy 3:1-4 (NIV)

In the ministry, it is important that you distance yourself from anything that resembles the love of money. Do not let money influence the decisions you take for the ministry.

5. If you love the Lord, you will not love your family so much: You cannot love two masters.

He that loveth father or mother more than me is not worthy of me: and he that loveth son or daughter more than me is not worthy of me.

Matthew 10:37

Jesus is always comparing the love you have for him with the love that you have for your family.

57

Your excessive love for family is proof that you do not love the Lord. That is why those who emphasize so much on loving the family have led the church into barrenness and emptiness. You will notice there are many preachers who teach so much about marriage and family. There are many people teaching about how to have a good family and a good life. What is the effect of this emphasis? It serves to dry out your love for God.

The word of God teaches us to love our families. Satan has caused us to overemphasize these teachings and this has led us away from our Lord.

6. If you love the Lord, you will not love yourself so much: You cannot love two masters.

This know also, that in the last days perilous times shall come. FOR MEN SHALL BE LOVERS OF THEIR OWN SELVES, covetous, boasters, proud, blasphemers, disobedient to parents, unthankful, unholy, Without natural affection, trucebreakers, false accusers, incontinent, fierce, despisers of those that are good, Traitors, heady, highminded, lovers of pleasures more than lovers of God

2 Timothy 3:1-4

Loving yourself so much proves that you do not love the Lord. You cannot serve yourself and serve the Lord. You have to choose between yourself and the Lord. People who love themselves cannot go on missions. People who love themselves cannot love God. Those who love themselves are selfish. They only think about themselves. They care for themselves. They go shopping for themselves. They plan things for themselves. They work hard for themselves. They make sacrifices for themselves.

On the other hand, they do not think about the Lord. They do not care for the church. They do not make any sacrifices for the ministry. They do not plan on how to serve the Lord and follow Him.

It is not easy to live with a selfish person. The selfishness of a person can minister hurt and pain to those who suffer from the person's self-centred life. How the Lord wishes that we would think about Him. How the Lord wishes that we would think about Him.

7. If you love the Lord, you will not love the world: You cannot love two masters:

Love not the world, neither the things that are in the world. If any man love the world, the love of the Father is not in him. For all that is in the world, the lust of the flesh, and the lust of the eyes, and the pride of life, is not of the Father, but is of the world.

1 John 2:15-16

Your love of the world proves that you do not love the Lord. If you love the Lord, you will flush out other loves. If you love the Lord, you will not love the world. Once the love of the world is found in you, the love of the Father is not in you.

A brother who loves the world, loves parties, music, money, riches, clubs, drinking, smoking, fooling, drugs, women, men, clothes and every other form of vanity.

Lovers of the world are lovers of success, wealth, large cities, metropolitan living, showy lifestyles, big houses, big cars, big parties, fantastic hotels and never-ending pleasure. Unfortunately, such people do not love the Lord at all. It is easy to see where their hearts are. If you love the Lord you will not love the world!

8. If you love the Lord, you will not give your love to women: You cannot love two masters.

But KING SOLOMON LOVED MANY STRANGE WOMEN, together with the daughter of Pharaoh, women of the Moabites, Ammonites, Edomites, Zidonians, and Hittites; Of the nations concerning which the Lord said unto the children of Israel, Ye shall not go in to them, neither shall they come in unto you: for surely they will turn away your heart after their gods: Solomon clave unto these in love. And he had seven hundred wives, princesses, and three hundred concubines: and his wives turned away his heart. For it came to pass, when Solomon was old, that his wives turned away his heart after other gods: and his heart was not perfect with the Lord his God, as was the heart of David his father. For Solomon went after Ashtoreth the goddess of the Zidonians, and after Milcom the abomination of the Ammonites. And Solomon did evil in the sight of the Lord, and went not fully after the Lord, as did David his father. Then did Solomon build an high place for Chemosh, the abomination of Moab, in the hill that is before Jerusalem, and for Molech, the abomination of the children of Ammon. And likewise did he for all his strange wives, which burnt incense and sacrificed unto their gods. And the Lord was angry with Solomon, because his heart was turned from the Lord God of Israel, which had appeared unto him twice,

1 Kings 11:1-9

Solomon's downturn happened when he gave himself to the love of women. The scripture tells us that he loved many strange women. Although he was the king and had all power to rule his kingdom, the women he loved destroyed his leadership. What exactly did the women do? Was Solomon destroyed because he had sex with all these women? Was he committing a sin when he married all these women? Apparently, polygamy was accepted in those days.

Then what power did the women have in his life? They had the power of influence! In order to prove his love to the myriad of women he encountered, he had to tell them secrets and promise them gifts and favours. The secrets that he gave away probably compromised his reign. The favours that he gave to these people probably compromised him.

Women have a subtle influence on the affairs of this world. If you do not have a proper respect for the influence that women have, you may live to regret it. You must have a proper respect for the influence that a wife can exert on your life. You must also have a proper respect for the influence that other women whom you are not married to can have on your life. Your life and ministry can change if you love any woman more than you should.

The Bible says the way of a man with a maiden is both strange and mysterious. Make sure that your mind is clear. Make sure that your feelings are not misleading you. Make sure that the gentle, attractive face of that lady is not misleading you and destroying your clear train of thought.

As long as you are part of this world, you will be influenced by women. Women abound everywhere. But the love of the Lord must be the biggest thing in your life. The success stories of ministry are always of men who did not live to please any man. They are stories of men who did not live to please any woman. You cannot please God and also please your wife. You cannot please God and also please a woman. You cannot please God and also please your friends.

But he that is married careth for the things that are of the world, how he may please his wife.

1 Corinthians 7:33

Samson was not destroyed by his wife! Samson was destroyed by a friend! Samson was not destroyed because he had sex with a woman. Samson was destroyed because he yielded to the influence and pressure that came on him from a woman.

And she said unto him, How canst thou say, I love thee, when thine heart is not with me? thou hast mocked me these three times, and hast not told me wherein thy great strength lieth.

Judges 16:15

Beware of the manipulations of a woman you love! Beware of the decisions you take because of a woman you love! Beware of giving your heart to a woman you love! Beware of loving your wife more than you love the Lord. You cannot love two masters. You cannot love two things. Let us focus on loving the Lord.

Truly, there is no other person that is worth loving as much as you love the Lord.

There is a door of destiny in the ministry. When you pass through that door you will not love any human being dearly again. You will love the Lord and you will love only people that the Lord wants you to love.

Every person you love, who becomes a rival to the Lord, will be a source of pain to you. God is a jealous God and He wants to own you and keep you to Himself! If you love the Lord, you will not love any other master. Let us love the Lord with all our hearts and put aside all challenges to this love.

CHAPTER 11

If You Love the Lord: You Will Have to Prove It

Wherefore shew ye to them, and before the churches, THE PROOF OF YOUR LOVE, and of our boasting on your behalf.

2 Corinthians 8:24

Why does love have to be proved? Love has to be proved because many people claim to love. Many people say, "I love you." "I love you" is now like a meaningless cliché. The phrase "I love you" is a statement that has long lost its impact, power and influence. The phrase, "I love you very much" is something that has lost its meaning.

God is tired of hearing our vain speeches. God is tired of hearing our meaningless love songs. I am sure He looks down from heaven and asks, "To what purpose are these songs? Are they not telling lies?" Almighty God asks, "Are they telling the truth or are they making fun of me when they say, 'I love you'?"

How do you prove your love? You prove your love by passing the tests of love. The test of love is the test of obedience. If you love the Lord you will obey His commandments. That is why you have to prove your love by passing the test of obedience. All through the Bible, we see God testing those who claim to love Him. There are a number of things that can be used to test your love for God. There are things that will happen to you that are simply tests. They are circumstances that have been thrown together and presented to you by the Lord. These events are to test you to see if you love the Lord.

Three Proofs of Love

1. Prove your love by obedience.

And said, "I swear by myself, declares the Lord, that because you have done this and have not withheld your son, your only son, I will surely bless you and make your descendants as numerous as the stars in the sky and as the sand on the seashore. Your descendants will take possession of the cities of their enemies,

Genesis 22:16-17

Abraham and the test of love: Abraham was called a friend of God. This is because He passed the test of obedience (which is the test of love). When Abraham agreed to sacrifice his son, he passed the greatest test of his life. It was the test of obedience, which is the test of love!

2. Prove your love by not following false prophets.

If there arise among you a prophet, or a dreamer of dreams, and giveth thee a sign or a wonder, And the sign or the wonder come to pass, whereof he spake unto thee, saying, Let us go after other gods, which thou hast not known, and let us serve them; THOU SHALT NOT HEARKEN UNTO THE WORDS OF THAT PROPHET, OR THAT DREAMER OF DREAMS: FOR THE LORD YOUR GOD PROVETH YOU, TO KNOW WHETHER YE LOVE THE LORD YOUR GOD with all your heart and with all your soul.

Deuteronomy 13:1-3

The Israelites were also made to pass through the test of love. God wanted to be sure if they really loved Him. Their test of love was the test of idolatry. Would they serve other idols? Would there be something else that would win their hearts? Would they fall for a side attraction? Would someone else be more important, more attractive, more interesting and more appealing to the Israelites? God wanted to know whether he was enough for them.

3. Prove your love by giving.

Wherefore shew ye to them, and before the churches, THE PROOF OF YOUR LOVE, and of our boasting on your behalf.

2 Corinthians 8:24

Giving is a test of love. Sometimes people claim to love you but when they have to give, they do not. I once asked some prosperous business people to support the ministry. When I asked them to give, they stuttered and mumbled an excuse about the economy and how things were difficult. These people were not prepared to give because they were full of excuses.

Indeed, giving is a reflection of how much you love God. God does not need what you have. Giving just proves your love for Him! If you love God you will give and give again. If you love the Lord you will not make excuses! If you love the Lord, you will pass the test of giving.

CHAPTER 12

If You Love the Lord: Expect These Blessings

In that I command thee this day to LOVE THE LORD thy God, to walk in his ways, and to keep his commandments and his statutes and his judgments, that thou mayest live and multiply: and THE LORD THY GOD SHALL BLESS THEE in the land whither thou goest to possess it.

Deuteronomy 30:16

1. If you love the Lord, you will experience His presence and His manifestations.

HE THAT HATH MY COMMANDMENTS, AND KEEPETH THEM, HE IT IS THAT LOVETH ME: AND HE THAT LOVETH ME SHALL BE LOVED OF MY FATHER, AND I WILL LOVE HIM, AND WILL MANIFEST MYSELF TO HIM. Judas saith unto him, not Iscariot, Lord, how is it that thou wilt manifest thyself unto us, and not unto the world? Jesus answered and said unto him, If a man love me, he will keep my words: and my Father will love him, and we will come unto him, AND MAKE OUR ABODE WITH HIM.

John 14:21-23

The manifestations of God's power in your life will increase as your love for God increases. The presence of God will be clearly evident as you grow in your love for God. Love is the most important commandment. As you love God and obey this greatest commandment, God returns your love by giving you the greatest thing that He can: His presence! The presence of God follows God-lovers.

God wants to be near those who love Him. Would you not prefer to be near your lovers? God wants to be near His lovers! Would you not visit your lovers more than you visit ordinary people? Would you not do more things for your lovers? Would you not show yourself more to your lovers? Of course, you would!

Watch out for the two greatest blessings that come to those who love the Lord: His presence and His manifestation! All through this chapter, you will see different manifestations that come to those who love the Lord. He will do for you things that eye has not seen nor ear heard. He will give you the corn, and the wine and the oil. He will give you the rain in its season. He will make you to shine like the sun in its full strength. You will be full of glory and strength because you love the Lord.

2. If you love the Lord, God will do things that are unheard of for you.

But as it is written, Eye hath not seen, nor ear heard, neither have entered into the heart of man, the things which God hath prepared for them that love him.

1 Corinthians 2:9

As you love the Lord, expect to experience things that you have not heard of or seen before. As I have served the Lord, I have seen churches that I have never heard of before. I have written books with titles that I have never seen before. As I have served the Lord, I have been to nations that I had never dreamt of going to. As I have served the Lord, I have eaten foods that I had never heard of.

As I have served the Lord, I have met with great men of God whom I never thought I would meet. As I have loved the Lord, I have found myself meeting with presidents of different nations and leading them to Christ. These are fantastic experiences which eye has not seen nor ear heard!

3. If you love the Lord, God will cause all things to work out for you.

And we know that all things work together for good to them that love God, to them who are the called according to his purpose.

Romans 8:28

This amazing scripture is quoted by people who assume that all things will naturally work out for good. Unfortunately, that is not the case. Many things do not just work out for good.

Also, this scripture is quoted by people who assume that, "All things work together for good for Christians!" They say, "All things work together for believers." They say, "All things work together for good for those who go to church. They say, "All things work together for good to those who are good." Indeed, none of these statements are true. The scripture actually says, "All things work together for good to those who love the Lord."

It is THOSE WHO LOVE THE LORD who have this blessing. It is an amazing miracle if all things do work together for good. You will receive this amazing blessing as you love the Lord.

In real life, many things actually work out badly. Everyone knows that! But all things will work together for good to those who love the Lord! When certain bad things happen, we lose hope and know that things will only get worse. The question on everyone's mind is, "How can this work out for good?" However, this amazing scripture stands as a beacon of hope for God-lovers. Expect all things to work out for good as you serve the Lord.

4. If you love the Lord, God will be with you in trouble and defend you in times of crises.

BECAUSE HE HATH SET HIS LOVE UPON ME, therefore will I deliver him: I will set him on high, because he hath known my name. He shall call upon me, and I will answer him: I WILL BE WITH HIM IN TROUBLE; I will deliver him, and honour him. With long life will I satisfy him, and shew him my salvation.

Psalm 91:14-16

Trouble comes to everyone in this life. There is no one who lives his life without seeing some kind of trouble. God did not promise that Christians would not have any trouble. But he promised to be with us in time of trouble. He says he will deliver you and honour you in the time of your difficulty. This promise is made to you because you love God!

This promise is not being made to you because you read the Bible. This promise is not made to you because you recite the Psalm. This promise is not made to you because you are a member of a church. Read it carefully: This promise is for those who have set their love on God.

5. If you love the Lord, you will be satisfied with long life and salvation.

BECAUSE HE HATH SET HIS LOVE UPON ME, therefore will I deliver him: I will set him on high, because he hath known my name. He shall call upon me, and I will answer him: I will be with him in trouble; I will deliver him, and honour him. With LONG LIFE will I satisfy him, and shew him my SALVATION.

Psalm 91:14-16

Long life and salvation are blessings that are promised to God-lovers. If you love God, you can expect to experience the blessings of long life and salvation. Many people who read the ninety-first Psalm do not experience long life and salvation. The fact that you have read this scripture and quote it often does not mean it will happen for you.

The condition for experiencing the blessing of long life and salvation is to love God. May you receive the blessing of long life! Whatever shortens your life is cursed! May heaven respond to your love for Almighty God! May you enjoy long life and salvation because you have set your love on Him!

I call heaven and earth to record this day against you, that I have set before you life and death, blessing and cursing: therefore choose life, that both thou and thy seed may live: That thou mayest LOVE THE LORD THY GOD, and that thou mayest obey his voice, and that thou mayest CLEAVE UNTO HIM: FOR HE IS THY LIFE, AND THE LENGTH OF THY DAYS: that thou mayest dwell in the land which the Lord sware unto thy fathers, to Abraham, to Isaac, and to Jacob, to give them.

Deuteronomy 30:19-20

6. If you love the Lord, and keep his commandments and He will show you great mercy.

Thou shalt have no other gods before me. Thou shalt not make unto thee any graven image, or any likeness of any thing that is in heaven above, or that is in the earth beneath, or that is in the water under the earth: Thou shalt not bow down thyself to them, nor serve them: for I the Lord thy God am a jealous God, visiting the iniquity of the fathers upon the children unto the third and fourth generation of them that hate me; AND SHEWING MERCY UNTO THOUSANDS OF THEM THAT LOVE ME, AND KEEP MY COMMANDMENTS.

Exodus 20:3-6

Mercy and love are deeply connected. God will show great mercy to people that love Him. If you are part of humanity, you will one day need mercy to be shown to you. To receive mercy is to have your sins forgotten and ignored as though they never happened.

Most people never have their sins forgotten. Through the blood of Jesus your sins will be washed away. But will they be forgotten? God promises you mercy because you love Him. When you stand before a person you have wronged, you will discover how your sins are not easily forgotten.

God promises to forgive and forget the sins of those who love him. God loves you back when you love Him!

I once met a man whose wife had been wretchedly unfaithful to him. Everyone who knew them was a hundred per cent sure that he would abandon his wife and divorce her. But he forgave her and showed her much affection and much love. With time, it became apparent that he really desired and loved his unfaithful wife. I understood that mercy is shown to those who are loved. He loved her and showed her great mercy. Mercy is always connected to love.

7. If you love the Lord, he will keep his covenant with you. No love no covenant! No promises work.

> Know therefore that the Lord thy God, he is God, the faithful God, WHICH KEEPETH COVENANT AND MERCY WITH THEM THAT LOVE HIM and keep his commandments to a thousand generations; And repayeth them that hate him to their face, to destroy them: he will not be slack to him that hateth him, he will repay him to his face.

Deuteronomy 7:9-10

God keeps covenant with those who love Him. Keeping covenant means that God does not change His mind. Do you want God to keep His promises to you? Do you want God to remain the same and not change his mind about you? It may interest you to know that God can change His mind! God has changed His mind before!

God made man to live forever but He changed His mind and sentenced him to death.

God made Adam and Eve and gave them a home in the garden of Eden. After Adam and Eve had a relationship with the devil, God changed His mind and took back His home. He did not want Adam and Eve to live there anymore. God put armed security guards in His home to prevent Adam and Eve, in particular, from coming there again.

God promised to take the Israelites to the Promised Land. But He changed His mind in the middle of the journey.

God made human beings to inhabit the earth. As men multiplied and became evil, God changed His mind and drowned the entire human race that He had made to fill the earth.

After the flood, there was nobody to inhabit the earth.

One day, there will be a good reason why God may have to change His mind about you. In that day, your love for God will really count. God will keep His covenant with the people that love Him. He will not change His mind towards people that have shown fervent love for Him.

It is important to be a God-lover. There are many important blessings for those who love God.

8. If you love the Lord, he will give you the former rain, the latter rain, the corn, the oil and the wine. Prosperity!

And it shall come to pass, if ye shall hearken diligently unto my commandments which I command you this day, TO LOVE THE LORD YOUR GOD, AND TO SERVE HIM WITH ALL YOUR HEART AND WITH ALL YOUR SOUL, THAT I WILL GIVE YOU THE RAIN OF YOUR LAND IN HIS DUE SEASON, THE FIRST RAIN AND THE LATTER RAIN, THAT THOU MAYEST GATHER IN THY CORN, AND THY WINE, AND THINE OIL. And I will send grass in thy fields for thy cattle, that thou mayest eat and be full.

Deuteronomy 11:13-15

The corn, the oil and the wine represent the blessings of God on Israel. God promised many blessings of sustenance for His people, if they loved Him. The three basic blessings of life were promised. Although it looks insignificant, the corn, the oil and the wine are the basis of all prosperity. Receive sustenance and prosperity as you love God!

9. If you love the Lord, you will live and multiply.

See, I have set before thee this day life and good, and death and evil; IN THAT I COMMAND THEE THIS DAY TO LOVE THE LORD THY GOD, TO WALK IN HIS WAYS, AND TO KEEP HIS COMMANDMENTS AND HIS STATUTES AND HIS JUDGMENTS, THAT THOU MAYEST LIVE AND MULTIPLY: and the Lord thy God shall bless thee in the land whither thou goest to possess it.

Deuteronomy 30:15-16

Living and multiplying is a blessing that is given to God's people. Many years ago, I started a church in a poor area of the city. As the years went by, God blessed the church and it grew. I do not think that I realised how much God had blessed me. I had taken the growth of the church for granted. I thought to myself; "all churches grow".

One day, after many years, I was driving through the same area and I saw a church that had a similar name to ours. I recognised that this church had been there for many years. The church was meeting in a wooden structure, which resembled more of a horse stable. I remembered when our church used to meet in such a structure that also resembled a horse stable. I realised that God had brought me very far and had caused me to live, to flourish and to multiply.

The Lord your God promises you the blessing of living and multiplying. All you have to do is to love Him and all these things will be manifest in your life.

10. If you love the Lord, you will shine like the sun in his full strength.

So let all thine enemies perish, O Lord: BUT LET THEM THAT LOVE HIM BE AS THE SUN WHEN HE GOETH FORTH IN HIS MIGHT. And the land had rest forty years.

Judges 5:31

As you love God, you will be like the sun shining in its full strength. The sun in its full strength is truly a glorious spectacle. You cannot even look at the sun when it is shining in its full strength. A God lover is blessed to be like the sun shining in its full strength. Glorious! Magnificent! Splendid! Wonderful! Outstanding! Celebrated! This is how you will be described because you are a God lover!

11. If you love the Lord, you are better than all the others.

And he shall be unto thee a restorer of thy life, and a nourisher of thine old age: for THY DAUGHTER IN LAW, WHICH LOVETH THEE, WHICH IS BETTER TO THEE THAN SEVEN SONS, hath born him.

Ruth 4:15

Naomi was told that her daughter-in-law who loved her was better than seven sons. This was a fact. One person can indeed be worth more than several other people. One child who loves you is better than all the other children who do not love you put together. Love increases your value! Love increases the value of a child! Love increases the value of a servant. Love increases the value of a human being. Someone who loves me is worth a hundred times more than someone who does not love me. A lawyer who loves me is worth more to me than a lawyer who is just doing a job. A doctor who loves me is worth a hundred times more than a doctor who is just doing a job. A nurse who loves me is worth a hundred times more than a nurse who is just doing a job.

Conclusion

There is no end to the blessings that follow true lovers!

There is also no end to the making of many books!

May the power and the anointing of the Holy Ghost make you into a God-lover!